Do You Know How Much Your Momma Loves You?

Sarah Boutte

for Emmett & Elise

Thank you to my sweet friend Jamie Campbell for your brilliance, insight, and encouragement.

Text and Illustration c 2017 **by Sarah Boutte**
All rights reserved
No part of this publication may be reproduced in whole or in part, or stored in a retrieval system, or transmitted in any form or by any means, electronic, mechanical, photocopying, recording, or otherwise, without expressed written consent and permission of the author.

ISBN 978-0-692-96434-7

Do you know how much your Momma loves you?

She loves you

BIG BIG

She may try to tell you in different ways...

She may say she loves you more than…
What is the biggest thing you can think of?

A T-Rex?
Well, she may say she loves you even bigger than that.

Or even bigger than the internet.

She may say she loves you bigger
than the whole city,

the whole ocean,

the whole sky,

bigger than the stars and back.

She may say she loves you bigger than a
road that never ends...

But it's actually MUCH, MUCH, MUCH more than that.

You see, something special happens
when a Momma gets a baby.

Her heart explodes!
She gets to have so much love for you, sweet child.
It's bigger than the whole world.
It's too big to describe.

It doesn't even fit on this page.

or this one…

or this one!

And if she gets another baby, it just happens all again.
She has all her love for you,
and all her love for your brother or sister too.
It can just keep happening and never run out.
Your Momma is so lucky.

Loving you is the
best gift.